"My observation has been; Jerry is a student of The Word and an out-of-the-box thinker. He has a God-given ability to not only understand Scripture, but also the wisdom to make that knowledge applicable in everyday life. His straight 'Bible Truth,' 'how-to,' 'hands-on' style of writing and teaching is so needed in our Churches today.

I have not only published his books, but have studied them along with my Bible, and now consider them an intregal part of my personal 'Faith Library.'

So it is my privilege to recommend to you this book and my friend Missionary Teacher and Author, Jerry Hollenbeck."

> Aaron D. Jones
> Artist, Minister, Publisher and
> Author of --
> - The Confessions of a Victorious Believer
> - Sound from Heaven
> - In the Secret Place of THE MOST HIGH

HAVING DONE ALL, TO STAND

STAND THEREFORE

HAVING DONE ALL, TO STAND

STAND THEREFORE

by
Jerry W. Hollenbeck

Christian Literature & Artwork
A BOLD TRUTH Publication

Unless otherwise indicated all Scripture quotations are taken from the King James Version of The Bible.

ISBN 13: 978-0-9965908-2-2

BOLD TRUTH PUBLISHING
300 West 41st Street
Sand Springs, Oklahoma 74063
www.BoldTruthPublishing.com

Contents

Section - NOTES

Kingdom Seekers
Featuring
Band of Believers Bible Study

Orientation

This is to be a concentrated, focused teaching for the express purpose of learning how to stand, without any frills or fillers to dazzle your minds. There is much to be said and I believe the Lord is showing me that I need to make this study as brief as possible, and not fill your minds with too much information. The more information, the more consideration. The more consideration, the more chance to be confused and misdirected.

The study will take on the same form as the **Kingdom Realities Bible Study** did. Week-1-Day-1 through…. who knows when we will stop.

Looking up Scripture references will be your responsibility. If you already know you won't do it, there's no reason for you to even start the study, you're not committed enough. If you're one of those who think they can handle whatever comes along on your own and you're okay with how life is treating you. You are indeed on your own.

For those of us who look to God as our source of help in time of need, and are teachable, buckle up. I'm not going to coddle anybody. I will speak to you as adults, hungry for the knowledge of God. *Prv. 4:20-23.*

I believe the Lord is going to take us to a place we've never been before. We're going to see things that we've never seen before, and hear things that we've never heard before! Why, because unto you, it is given to know the mysteries of the Kingdom of God, but to them that are without, it is not given. This is going to be a no-nonsense Bible study aimed at people that are fed up with not being fed up. God has made us a Way, and until we learn The Way, we will live out our lives like we always have, "The School of Hard Knocks." Compounded by Murphy's Law, "if anything can go wrong, it will!!"

We're going to be shooting from the hip through the eye of Faith at a target that cannot be seen by the natural eye. We will be looking at things that are spiritual that only the mind of Christ will be able to discern. Also, we will cop an attitude that we have never exhibited before.

We will gain the confidence to get in the enemy's face and drive him out of our affairs.

1 Jo. 5:14 And this is the confidence that we have in him,.... when we are finished, and are looking back, we will see that standing against the wiles of the devil is little more than child's play,…if you know how!! But if you don't know how, it's impossible to stand!!

> *Romans 8:6*
> *For to be carnally minded is death; but to be spiritually minded is life and peace.*

God is not going to override your will. *Ro. 8:6* simply means that if you want to go it alone; God will not interfere. You are still saved, but without God's help or influence in the world.

Matthew 11:28-30
28. Come unto me, all ye that labour and are heavy laden, and I will give you rest.

29. Take my yoke upon you, and learn of me; for I am meek and lowly in heart: and ye shall find rest unto your souls.

30. For my yoke is easy, and my burden is light.

Ephesians 4:14
Wherefore he saith, Awake thou that sleepest, and arise from the dead, and Christ shall give thee light.

Romans 8:29
For whom he did foreknow, he also did predestinate to be conformed to the image of his Son.

OK, we see the mandate, now, LET'S DO IT!!

Kingdom Seekers
Featuring
Band of Believers Bible Study

Introduction

An issue has come up that commands some attention in these last of the last days. Having done all to stand, is something that we have not been doing. It's easy to prove. Just check out the long lines when a healing invitation is given in our churches. Small churches have many come forward to be healed, large churches have hundreds to come forward to be healed. There's something wrong with this picture. We have not been being taught how to stand!! Since we don't know how to stand, how can we possibly STAND THEREFORE? …AWKWARD!!

A few months ago I completed a Bible study on facebook called **Kingdom Realities,** you can find it on the **"Kingdom Seekers International"** page. That study deals with Kingdom laws, principles, and truths that we can put into practice in the here and now to overcome our short comings, conditions, tests, and trials, not having to wait for the great by and by, we can apply these laws and principles against our circumstances in the here and now, and overcome them by using the Word of God.

The study was easy to post on Facebook because the Lord helped me develop it six years ago and all I had to do was write each lesson daily for three months. This study however, is going to be fresh manna, so to speak. This issue, "having done all to stand" has not been addressed yet by this ministry or by our churches. The long healing lines make this unfortunate truth self evident.

The Band of Believers Bible Study is at this time, open ended. I don't know how long it will take to complete. **The Kingdom Realities Bible Study** was easy. I knew it would be twelve weeks long. Starting with Week-1-Day-1 to Week-12-Day-5. **The Band of Believers** will start with Week-1-Day-1, but the path it will take remains to be seen.

The Kingdom Realities Study has been put into book form. The name of the book is **"The Kingdom of God, An Agrarian Society."** It is in a large work-book format. Band of Believers will also be published in book form.

We will be using *Eph. 6:12-17* as our foundation passage of scripture.

> *12. For we wrestle not against flesh and blood, but against principalities, against powers, against the rulers of the darkness of this world, against spiritual wickedness in high places.*
>
> *13. Wherefore take unto you the whole armour of God, that ye may be able to withstand in the evil day, and having done all, to stand.*
>
> *14. Stand therefore, having your loins girt about with truth, and having on the breastplate of righteousness;*
>
> *15. And your feet shod with the preparation of the gospel of peace;*

16. Above all, taking the shield of faith, wherewith ye shall be able to quench all the fiery darts of the wicked.

17. And take the helmet of salvation, and the sword of the Spirit, which is the word of God:

I hope you are as interested and as excited as I am. I can hardly wait to see where the Lord will take us in this study. I also hope you get on board right away because where we're going may as well be light years away from all we have come to know in this life as a Christian on planet earth.

I will say this, when we learn of the power of the Kingdom, healing school will suddenly become obsolete. Why? Because we will have done all to stand through the knowledge of God, imparted in this study, and now,… we can STAND THEREFORE!! That's why the Bible teaches us to renew our minds. *[Ro. 12:2; Eph. 5:14; Php. 2:5; Col. 3:10; 2 Tim. 2:5-8; Heb. 6:1-3]*

So what are we supposed to be renewing our minds from, and what are we supposed to be renewing our minds to? How about this, from the world's thoughts and ways, to God's thoughts and ways.

Though I don't consider "I have arrived" yet. Standing where I am right now, I see that we don't even know how to think yet, much less speak words and form sentences that will fill our needs and drive off the things that we don't want.

Everybody thinks that God is in charge!! Let me

burst that bubble right now. We,…are in charge!! Jesus put it this way,

> *Matthew 10:24-25a*
> *24. The disciple is not above his master, nor the servant above his lord.*
> *25. It is enough for the disciple that he be as his master, and the servant as his lord.*

> *Luke 6:40*
> *The disciple is not above his master: but every one that is perfect shall be as his master.*

Go ahead and look these scriptures up for yourselves. Your Bible "should" say the same thing. Are you a disciple? Do you consider yourself a servant?

■ **WEEK 1** ■

Band of Believers Bible Study
► Week-1-Day-1 ◄

"Blinded Minds"

2 Corinthians 4:4
In whom the god of this world hath blinded the minds of them which believe not

Our minds were blinded before we ever knew anything about God, or that there even was a God.

When we were born of Mom & Dad, we came into the world with nothing and we didn't know anything about God. We didn't even know that there was a God. If a person dies before he or she reaches the age of reason, that is to say, being innocent of the knowledge of good and evil, their spirit and soul will go back to God (where they came from.) After reaching the age of reason, knowing the difference between good and evil, the sin nature takes over and now, they're minds are blinded to the things of God, and now, they need the saviour Christ Jesus.

My point is this, everybody, even God's very own elect, had their minds blinded from the things of God, including you and me. That's why we need to be renewed in the spirit of our minds, that we might prove what is that good, acceptable, and perfect will of God for our lives.

The natural man, our flesh and blood bodies with a

brain and the ability to think and speak have nothing to do with the things of God.

1 Corinthians 2:9-16

9. But as it is written, Eye hath not seen, nor ear heard, neither have entered into the heart of man, the things which God hath prepared for them that love him.

10. But God hath revealed them unto us by his Spirit: for the Spirit searcheth all things, yea, the deep things of God.

11. For what man knoweth the things of a man, save the spirit of man which is in him? even so the things of God knoweth no man, but the Spirit of God.

12. Now we have received, not the spirit of the world, but the spirit which is of God; that we might know the things that are freely given to us of God.

13. Which things also we speak, not in the words which man's wisdom teacheth, but which the Holy Ghost teacheth; comparing spiritual things with spiritual.

14. But the natural man receiveth not the things of the Spirit of God: for they are foolishness unto him: neither can he know them, because they are spiritually discerned.

15. But he that is spiritual judgeth all things, yet he himself is judged of no man.

16. For who hath known the mind of the Lord, that he may instruct him? But we have the mind of Christ.

John 6:63
It is the spirit that quickeneth; the flesh prof-
iteth nothing: the words that I speak unto you,
they are spirit, and they are life.

The natural mind of reason cannot see into the things
of God. It is only the mind of the spirit, that can discern
spiritual things. That is to say, the mind of Christ. We
have a natural mind and we have a spiritual mind. Right
now, you may be dominated by the mind of the flesh, but
as you mature, you will become dominated by your spiritual mind which is able to discern spiritual things. Having
done all to stand is a process, not an instant breakthrough.

Colossians 3:10
And have put on the new man, which is re-
newed in knowledge after the image of him that
created him:

When we were born again spiritually, we received
what the Bible calls, the mind of Christ, which is a spiritual mind, able to discern spiritual things. *[Mk. 4:11-*
12; Jo. 3:3-6, 6:63; 1 Co. 2:9-16]
We need to know and understand that we were in
God once. *Eph. 1:4-5 (vs. 4) chosen us in him before the*
foundation of the world. (vs. 5) Having predestinated us
unto the adoption of children
Even though we are the very elect, someone had to

come and preach Christ to us. Our carnal mind was blinded, but when we received Jesus as saviour, we received the mind of Christ, and are NOW ABLE TO DISCERN, PERCEIVE, AND UNDERSTAND, the spiritual things of God, comparing spiritual things with spiritual. This doesn't mean that we **do** discern, perceive, and understand, it only means that we now **can**. We first,… must renew our minds.   *[Ro. 12:2; 1 Co. 2:5, 2:13-14; Eph. 4:23; Col. 3:10]*

So what am I saying? The minds of the unbelievers were blinded. Guess what? You were an unbeliever once. Your natural mind, the mind of reason was blinded from the things of God. In case you haven't noticed God is not going to renew your mind automatically. He has told you to do it and if you don't do it, it won't get done.

We cannot speak Spiritually, until we learn how to think Spiritually. All we know at the time of the new birth is what we have learned in the world through the mind of reason. Now,…we have to learn how God thinks and how God does things. Only then,…can we think and speak as our Heavenly Father does. Jesus said, My words, they are Spirit and they are life. We need to grow to the point that **our words**, they are Spirit and they are life. No one has ever been drug into the Kingdom of God, kicking and screaming. No one has ever sauntered into the knowledge of the Kingdom by accident either. We must press in! *[Jo. 8:31-32]* Are you a disciple? Do you want to be used, do you want to be an example for others, press in; take your place in God's plan. Stand up and be counted. A city on a hill cannot be hid. Be a shining example of the life that God has planed for His people. Time is running out. The end of time as we know it is at hand. I believe God is looking for a few good men and women to lead the way and show forth the manifold wisdom of God. Do we have to do this? No! But the gifts and callings of God are without repentance. We are qualified, but to answer the call is our own choice. Can we do it, YES!! WILL WE? Well,…that remains to be seen.

If any man have ears to hear, let him hear.

Do you remember what Jesus said about eunuchs in *Mt. 19:11-12*? Those things were written only for those who could receive it. *[Eph. 1:1-23; Col. 1:1-29]*

This Bible study is being written for those who can receive it.

Jesus is calling, COME UP HIGHER!!

Can you answer the call? All that needs to be done is to make a quality decision to press in, into the knowledge of God and learn how to think like God thinks and do things the same way God does things, much like you did when you learned how to live life in this natural realm from Mom and Dad.

Now,…we need to learn how to live in this Spiritual realm from our Heavenly Father.

Can we do this? YES!! Will it be easy? Jesus put it this way, for those who receive the Word, some THIRTY fold, some SIXTY, and some an HUNDRED. It could very well be, as your several ability, or, as you can receive it!! Receive what? Knowledge, insight, and understanding, and after that,…exercise Wisdom.

Band of Believers Bible Study
► Week-1-Day-2 ◄

"Girt about with Truth"

Ephesians 6:10-17

(vs. 14) *Stand therefore, having your loins girt about with truth...*

John 8:31-32
31. If ye continue in my word, then are ye my disciples indeed;
32. And ye shall know the truth, and the truth shall make you free.

So many people misquote this scripture. They say, the truth will "set" you free. That denotes an instant result, but the scripture says, the truth shall "make" you free. That, denotes a time, or process. We live in an agrarian society. We sow, and then we reap the fruit of what we have sown. We have a most excellent opportunity, over and above what man's knowledge can give us. We have the privilege to deal with exact knowledge. Knowledge that is so exact, so accurate that it qualifies to be a truth. A truth so exact, so accurate, so true that it qualifies to be a law. Why? Because God said it, established it, and set it in motion for us to use in time of need.

Mk. 4:14 The sower soweth the word. The soil we sow in is the hearts of men, or our own hearts.

(vs. 15) *...the word that was sown in their hearts.*

> John 17:17
> *Sanctify them through thy truth: thy word is truth.*

Since the truth comes in the form of Words, everything God says is able to bare the fruit of what is said. The only rate of exchange in the Spirit realm is words,... spoken with forethought, and intent. Not money, not silver, not gold,...it's words only in The Kingdom of God. In other words, we need to learn to mean what we say. Sowing our words as seeds like God was doing in *Genesis 1:1-31*. God's Word is alive and well able to produce itself on our behalf. We can see it clearly in...

> Isaiah 55:10-11
> *10. For as the rain cometh down, and the snow from heaven, and returneth not thither, but watereth the earth, and maketh it bring forth and bud, that it may give seed to the sower, and bread to the eater:*
> *11. So shall my word be that goeth forth out of my mouth: it shall not return unto me void, but it shall accomplish that which I please, and it shall prosper in the thing whereto I sent it.*

God's Word is designed to produce what it says or describes. He has placed the power to produce itself "in the words, or in the promises" just as a seed is designed to produce "itself." We see in Genesis, that every seed produces after its own kind. The promises of God, recorded in the Bible are seeds, designed to produce what they say or describe, but there is a qualifier here.

These seeds need to be planted by Faith, accompanied with thought and intent because the Word, Jesus, is in you. He is quick and powerful, and is a discerner of the thoughts and intents of the heart. And that's not all. After we have prayed, or sown the seed, now we need to be in a mode of expectation. If we are expecting what we prayed for will actually happen, that's Faith, and Jesus will confirm that word, or promise, or what we asked for in His name, with signs following.

If we are not expecting it to come to pass, Jesus is not obligated to confirm that Word or promise even though that Word, or promise has all the potential to produce the fruit of what was said and/or what the Word or promise described.

Do you see the inference? Jesus in Genesis did everything God said. The worlds were created by Jesus, "the Word." whereas now,…the "Word" lives in you just as the Word lived in God in Genesis. Think about that for a minute. The Word of God lives in you. Yeah but it's Jesus that lives in us!! Well who do you think Jesus is? The "Word" made flesh.

John 14:13-14

13. And whatsoever ye shall ask in my name, "that will I do," that the Father may be glorified in the Son.

14. If ye shall ask any thing in my name, "I will do it."

Do you want a microwave oven? A home, or a safe dependable car? Would you like to have your own business? Speak it, frame it with words, just like God framed the creation in Genesis. Believe what you said "shall" come to pass!! Jesus said, you will have what you said. I didn't say it, Jesus said it!! But first we must learn how to think like God thinks and then learn how to form words and sentences and speak correctly. That falls under the category of,

"Having done all to Stand."

God's truth will produce itself after we learn how to direct it. How did Jesus put it? What things soever you desire, when you pray, believe you receive them, and you shall have them. To the carnal mind of reason, that sounds ridiculous, but to the mind of the Spirit, knowing how things are done in the Spirit realm, it is right and proper.

In the natural realm, all things start, or begin in the imagination. First the thought, then the thought is spoken or described, then it gets drawn on paper as a blue-print. Then earth movers come in and prepare the ground. Then the foundation is laid, then the walls, then the plumbing and electrical lines are put in, and so on,…Right?

In the Spirit realm we do things differently. Listen up, this is a truth!! There is no money in the Spirit realm, so we buy without money. We provide without bricks and mortar, lumber, plumbing pipe, or electrical wiring.

So how do we get things done? The same way God does! We speak what we want, doubt not in our heart, but believe what we said shall come to pass. Jesus said, when we do that,…we will have what we said!! Without money, and without price.

> *Isaiah 55:1-2*
>
> *1. Ho, every one that thirsteth, come ye to the waters, and he that hath no money; come ye, buy, and eat; yea, come, buy wine and milk without money and without price.*
>
> *2. Wherefore do ye spend money for that which is not bread? and your labour for that which satisfieth not? hearken diligently unto me, and eat ye that which is good, and let your soul delight itself in fatness.*

Did you catch it? We buy without money and without price. It's words only in The Kingdom of God. That is to say, words spoken with forethought and intent, meaning that what we said,… should actually come to pass.

Once you get on the other side of this learning curve, Faith will become little more than child's play, when you learn how to use it!!

Necessity,…is the mother of invention.

What do you need? What do you want? Frame it with words like God framed the creation in Genesis, **expecting**, until your words come to pass. That's Faith!! If you're not **expecting**, your not in Faith,…believing **for** what you said.

The church teaches that we work six days and rest the seventh. Why? Because *Gen. 2:1-2* teaches it to be so. However, *Heb. 4:1-10* teaches another thing. When God finished His works, He entered into rest. What were His works? His Sayings!! When God speaks, The Word,… goes out and performs the doing of what God said. That is to say, the second person of the Godhead, we now call Jesus. Jesus is the Word of God personified. In the book of Revelation Jesus will be given His new Name. guess what it is,…The Word of God. Jesus will take up His primary identity. He is, was, and always will be "The Word of God."

When we speak a Promise, Truth, or Spiritual law, Jesus is there, standing at the ready to perform the doing of what we said. However, we need to remember that our words need to be accompanied with thought and intent, in order for Jesus to confirm our words with signs following. We need to mean what we say,…we need to intend,…what we say shall surely come to pass!!

John 14:13-14

13. And whatsoever ye shall ask in my name, that will I do, that the Father may be glorified in the Son.

14. If ye shall ask any thing in my name, I will do it.

Just like in Genesis chapter One!!

As you grow in the knowledge of God, you will eventually see that you can put your name in Isa.55:11. So shall my word be that goeth forth out of my mouth: it shall not return unto me void, but it shall accomplish that which I please, and it shall prosper in the thing whereto I sent it.

So shall Ricky's word be, so shall Robert's word be, so shall Jennifer's word be,…anybodies name that has ears to hear this message. Can anybody do it? Well, we're all a product of what we've been taught. Sadly NO, not everyone will walk in the power of the Kingdom.

Band of Believers Bible Study
► Week-1-Day-3 ◄

"Principalities and Powers"

Ephesians 6:12
For we wrestle not against flesh and blood, but against principalities, against powers, against the rulers of the darkness of this world, against spiritual wickedness in high places.

We need to get this into our understanding that our fight is not with the city fathers, the school board, the bank's policies, the government, or any such thing. Our fight is with principalities, powers and rulers of darkness in high places.

We have authority over the earth, and the devil and his bunch, not men. You are not going to change your husband. You are not going to change your wife. So,…ask the Lord to **"change me."** We do not have authority over another person's free will, and right to choose!! We do however have authority over another person's body to cast out sickness, disease, aches and pains. We have authority to do the same in our own bodies as well. Our fight or plan of resistance is to stand against the wiles of the devil and his bunch according to God's promises, truths, and Spiritual laws.

James 4:7

Submit yourselves therefore to God. Resist the devil, and he will flee from you.

We need to cop an attitude. If what's going on around us lines up with the Word, and is counted a blessing, it is of God!! If what's going on out there doesn't line up with the Word, we need to reject it immediately, and consider it of the devil. The Bible is our measuring stick while we are still on this earth. *[Heb. 5:12-14]* We are growing! We are not unskillful in the "Word of Righteousness." We are ready and hungry for the strong meat of the Word of God!!

Some think I'm too harsh, too blunt, and even rude. Well that's Ok, you see I've copped an attitude and it's working for me. What I'm trying to do here is to cause you to cop an attitude too.

I repeat myself a lot in these teachings. I know that! But it is scriptural,

Isaiah 28:9-13

9. Whom shall he teach knowledge? and whom shall he make to understand doctrine? them that are weaned from the milk, and drawn from the breasts.

10. For precept must be upon precept, precept upon precept; line upon line, line upon line; here a little, and there a little:

11. For with stammering lips and another tongue will he speak to this people.

12. To whom he said, This is the rest wherewith ye may cause the weary to rest; and this is the refreshing: yet they would not hear.

13. But the word of the LORD was unto them precept upon precept, precept upon precept; line upon line, line upon line; here a little, and there a little; that they might go, and fall backward, and be broken, and snared, and taken.

Our pastors have to preach an acceptable message for all to hear. I'm directing my messages to those who want to be used and are hungry for the meat of the Word of God. People who can adopt a no-nonsense attitude, get in the devil's face and drive him out of their affairs.

It's impossible for God to lie, AND, He watches over His Word to perform it. Get that into your thinking.

My job, as I see it is to change the way people think. If I can change the way you think, you will change the way you speak. With your loins girt about with truth, you can stand against the wiles of the devil. Duuuh. Do you know what *Heb. 2:1-4* says?

Hebrews 2:1-4

1. Therefore we ought to give the more earnest heed to the things which we have heard, lest at any time we should let them slip.

2. For if the word spoken by angels was stedfast, and every transgression and disobedience received a just recompense of reward;

3. How shall we escape, if we neglect so great

salvation; which at the first began to be spoken by the Lord, and was confirmed unto us by them that heard him;

4. God also bearing them witness, both with signs and wonders, and with divers miracles, and gifts of the Holy Ghost, according to his own will?

Then *Hebrews 5:12-14*

12. For when for the time ye ought to be teachers, ye have need that one teach you again which be the first principles of the oracles of God; and are become such as have need of milk, and not of strong meat.

13. For every one that useth milk is unskilful in the word of righteousness: for he is a babe.

14. But strong meat belongeth to them that are of full age, even those who by reason of use have their senses exercised to discern both good and evil.

Let's get out of our comfort zones. Whatever is going on in your life right now,...what does that have to do with eternal life? Our Father God has made a way for us to overcome the circumstances in our lives, let's learn from Him about that!!

Matthew 6:33
But seek ye first the kingdom of God, and his righteousness; and all these things shall be added unto you.

What was Jesus talking about? What are we going

to eat, what are we going to drink, wherewithal shall we be clothed? The issues of life!! *[Prv. 4:20-23, Mt. 12:33-37]* Out of the heart, are the issues of life. Out of the heart, the mouth speaks. What are you saying about your circumstances? What would you like to say about them? Speak boldly!!

If you knew that you are in charge of your life, things would be different, way different wouldn't they? You bet they would.

Hey Bubba, you are indeed in charge of your life,…. BY CHRIST JESUS,…. "THE WORD."

Example:

> *Philippians 4:19*
> *But my God shall supply all your need according to his riches in glory by Christ Jesus.*

Did you notice, God does this according to His bank account, NOT YOURS? And He does it by Christ Jesus? Well,…who is Christ Jesus? The Word of God,…personified!!

SO, God meets our needs according to His riches, by the Word!!

We've all heard that "it" is not our fight, it's God's. God will fight for us. God will go before us. Well, how does He do it?

Let's use another example.

> *Isaiah 45:2-4*
> *2. I will go before thee, and make the crooked*

places straight: I will break in pieces the gates of brass, and cut in sunder the bars of iron:

3.And I will give thee the treasures of darkness, and hidden riches of secret places, that thou mayest know that I, the LORD, which call thee by thy name, am the God of Israel.

4. For Jacob my servant's sake, and Israel mine elect, I have even called thee by thy name: I have surnamed thee, though thou hast not known me.

One might say that God was speaking that to Cyrus!! OH? Well yes, He was, but, …are you not anointed? Are you not Israel, God's elect? Come on Church. God is speaking this about His people, of which you are one!

As we speak God's Word in the form of one of the promises, truths, or Spiritual laws, God goes before us making the way straight, and smooth, bringing down the high places, and bringing up the low places and we walk through the fiery trial without even the smell of smoke on us if we believe, and exercise Faith, Expecting!! If we don't, …we need to hunker down and prepare ourselves for a rough ride through the circumstances, enough said?

Band of Believers Bible Study
► Week-1-Day-4 ◄

"God's Provision, to the Intent"

Ephesians 3:1-21

*(vs. 10) To the intent that now unto the principalities and powers in heavenly places might be known **by the church** the manifold wisdom of God.*

We've been set up, literally!! Not in a bad way like the devil is trying to do to us, but in a most excellent way, by our Father God. We saw this before in the Kingdom Realities Study, 'Week-10-Day-5, "An Hostile Takeover."

God, at some point in time, before He created man, said some things and put them in motion for us to use in time of need. The Bible doesn't say this in so many words, but the Bible does say in *Heb. 4:3*, that the works were finished before the foundation of the world. What works was that? Well what was God doing in Genesis? He was framing the creation and restoration with Words. Right? That, was God's works. What we're looking at right now is what God must have said even before Genesis, or at least before He created man. Before the foundation of the world does not refer to the earth, or the universe, it refers to Mankind, or the inhabitants of the creation.

[Mt. 18:18-19, 21:21-22; Mk. 11:23-24; Lk. 17:6; Jo. 14:13-14, 15:7, 16:23-24]

God must have said words to set-up and establish these promises, or laws before He made man so that when man was created, these promises and laws would already be in place for us,… the works were finished before the foundation of the world!! Before I leave this paragraph, let me say this, when we pray the promise that covers our need, we too have finished our work, enter into the God kind of rest, expecting, until the promise comes to pass. IF, WE'RE BELIEVING FOR IT!! If we're not believing for it, forget it!!

God's intent is for us to learn how to live by our words, like He does. He gave us what to say, and a way to say it that will activate it, and bring it to pass in our life situations, tests, and trials. The promises are God's "intent" to save us from our problems. We do the speaking, Jesus backs us up by confirming the Words we speak with signs following, God also bearing us witness with signs and wonders and gifts of the Holy Ghost. [Mk. 16:20; Heb. 2:1-4]

Our work is to speak the promise, stand back, enter into rest, expecting until our words come to pass. Why? Because we finished from our works, as God did from His!!!!!!!!! Can you see it? The simplicity of it? When you're on the other side of the learning curve, Faith is child's play. For believers only? NO!! Anybody can do this, these are Spiritual Laws. All of mankind, including Christians, are living in the sum of our words, right now!! That's why we need to renew our minds to God's ways of doing things.

For those who are walking in the power of the Kingdom, there is no longer a need for healing school. No need for financial meetings. No national day of prayer meetings. No scheduled Tuesday night prayer meetings. We are all kings and priests, in charge and in control of our lives because of what God has prepared for us to walk in, before He even created us!! Can we all do this? Yes! Will we all do this? Probably not, but it won't be because it wasn't available to every one of us. Some just don't do it, that's all.

Anything, and I mean anything that can come against mankind on the earth has been covered by the promises of God. If you can't find a promise that covers your need, we have some exceeding great and precious promises to fall back on that will cover anything.

[Mt. 18:18-19, 21:21-22; Mk. 11:23-24; Lk. 17:6; Jo. 14:13-14, 15:7, 16:23-24]

We saw these earlier but it would behoove you to look at them again. They will address all your needs in life. Cars, trucks, homes, a college education for you and/or your children, boats, microwave ovens, multi million dollar ministry headquarters. ALL, and I mean ALL, without money and without price. Why? Because it's words only,… in The Kingdom of God.

Not all things that are conceived in the imagination end up being manifested in the natural realm. Only those things that we doubt not in our hearts, but believe for. Yes, they will be made manifest in this natural realm.

We are creative beings. Even the heathen who have not been born-again. Man, like God, is a creative being. Man was created in God's image and after His likeness. If we put a pair of Elk in a valley, wait a hundred years, all we would have at the end of that time is a very large herd of Elk.

If we put a man and a woman in a valley and wait for a hundred years, we would see homes, railroads, telephone polls, schools, automobiles, cell phones, computers, and I-pads. Why? Because we were created that way, in God's image, after His likeness. The sin nature of man was man's doing, not God's.

So God provided a saviour, to the intent, to reconcile man back to Himself. We are all born-again, "in Him." God said in,

> *Jeremiah 1:5*
> *Before I formed thee in the belly I knew thee; and before thou camest forth out of the womb I sanctified thee, and I ordained thee a prophet unto the nations.*

We all came out from God, died, because of the sin nature, and through God's provision for salvation, we were born again "in Him." God could have created a being to save the world, but He was not going to trust our never dying spirits to someone else. He came, in the form of a man and He died, taking our place on the cross.

> *John 1:14*
> *And the Word was made flesh, and dwelt among us, (and we beheld his glory, the glory as of the only begotten of the Father,) full of grace and truth.*

We really need to learn to live by our words. Words,... are the only rate of exchange in The Kingdom of God.

We are not alive today at random or by mistake. Read *Eph. 1:1-23*. We were foreknew and predestinated for this point in human history. Let your light so shine.

Band of Believers Bible Study
► Week-1-Day-5 ◄
"To The Intent"

Ephesians 3:1-21

> *(vs. 10) To the intent that now unto the principalities and powers in heavenly places might be known by the church the manifold wisdom of God.*

This chapter is written to Gentiles so that they would know that we too are included in God's plan of salvation from the foundation of the world. "To the intent," is a key phrase in understanding how the Word works. Jesus Himself came to us in *Jo. 14:13-14*. And said,...

> *13. And whatsoever ye shall ask in my name, that will I do, that the Father may be glorified in the Son.*
> *14. If ye shall ask any thing in my name, "I will do it."*

So we see that Jesus will not only do everything that God says, but He will also do what "we" say, in His Name.

The Word of God is now in our hearts, He knows what we're thinking, and He knows what we intend to do after the manifestation comes. Jesus, the Word of God, is in us, and He knows whether we're believing "for" what we're praying for or not. Therefore, to the intent, comes into play.

Jesus said it this way,

>Matthew 21:22
>And all things, whatsoever ye shall ask in prayer, believing, ye shall receive.

The word believing, denotes intent! He could have used the word expecting, or intending, ye shall receive. Again, He is in us, He knows if we're believing for something or not. If we're believing for it, intending for it, and expecting it, He's going to do *Mk. 16:20*. Yes, He will be working with us confirming the Word, with signs following. If we're not believing for it, our words will fall to the ground and Jesus is not obligated to confirm our words with signs following!!

I know that this sounds kind of involved but we need to learn how to pray effectively. Think of it as when you learned how to drive a car. All the things you had to know, all the things you had to look out for, in front of you, behind you, to either side, and above, and below. Learning to drive took time and effort, but now, you can drive to LA. or New York, without thinking. Why? Because you know how to drive a car.

Our prayers need to have certain parts, or ingredients in them. You've heard the term, shop like you mean it! We need to pray like we mean it. Our prayers need to include: thought, intent, purpose, and expectation. We pray, to the intent,… Faith, activates our prayers. Faith makes them work. If you're expecting the answer to come, that's Faith!! If your not expecting, you're not in Faith!! Pray according to the promises, you can't go wrong.

> *1 John 5:14-15*
> *14. And this is the confidence that we have in him, that, if we ask any thing according to his will, he heareth us:*
> *15. And if we know that He hear us, whatsoever we ask, we know that we have the petitions that we desired of Him.*

What could be more appropriate than praying the promises? The promises are God's will for His people. Duuuh.

When we speak, we must speak with conviction. We must learn to live by our words.

REVIEWING WEEK 1
Answers on bottom of page 71

1. After you become a Christian, who is responsible for renewing your mind?_____

2. We cannot speak Spiritually, until we do what? ____
_____

Explain? _____
_____
_____

3. Just as a seed is designed to produce "itself," God has placed that power to produce itself where? _____
_____

4. When a Christian is not expecting the answer or the promise to come, Jesus is not what? _____
Why, please explain?_____
_____
_____

5. Who is our fight with?_____
_____

How do we fight? _____
_____
_____

6. We need to learn to live by what? _____

7. "_____" is a key phrase in understanding how the Word works.

◾ WEEK 2 ◾

Band of Believers Bible Study
► Week-2-Day-1 ◄

"Casting Down Imaginations"

In spite of what we see, hear, taste, smell, or feel, the Word reigns supreme. The Word, can and will supersede any experience in this natural realm. Even nature itself. I heard on TV just last week, the laws of physics are falling apart. New data has changed even the most established laws that man has come up with and/or discovered.

God's laws, (I'm not talking about the law of Moses) were established from before the world was. (*Heb. 4:1-12*) God's knowledge is exact knowledge. Truth. When God speaks, it is not a suggestion, but a command, and what He says is so established, it becomes LAW!! Why? Because God decreed it, and it stands forever!!

We have been given the righteousness of God, which is the righteousness that Jesus established when He was on the earth, perfect, without spot or blemish or any such thing. There are things that accompany righteousness.

#1. Right standing with God, as though we had never sinned.

#2. We have the right and privilege to be partakers of the divine nature. What is that? We have the right to speak truth, and expect the truth to come to pass in our lives just like in Genesis, when God said, and it was so. And God saw that it was good.

All we have in the Kingdom of God is Words, to work with. No tools, no supplies, just words.

If we knew that we are in charge things would be different, wouldn't they? That's why the devil has blinded our minds, he doesn't want us to know that we are indeed in charge of our lives. We have the right to dictate policy in our own lives.

When things go wrong, God has given us instruction to do something about it.

> *2 Corinthians 10:3-6*
> *3. For though we walk in the flesh, we do not war after the flesh:*
> *4. (For the weapons of our warfare are not carnal, but mighty through God to the pulling down of strong holds;)*
> *5. Casting down imaginations, and every high thing that exalteth itself against the knowledge of God, and bringing into captivity every thought to the obedience of Christ;*
> *6. And having in a readiness to revenge all disobedience, when your obedience is fulfilled.*
>
> *(vs. 5) Casting down imaginations, and every high thing that exalteth itself against the knowledge of God.*

(That is to say, casting down thoughts, and natural things like the doctor's report, or anything else that goes against the established decrees of God, in His promises to us.

Yea, hath God not said? That's the flip chart game that the devil plays with our minds. Yea, hath God not said, and then he perverts what God has said, and changes it into something else. "You will not surely die."

The promises, are a most excellent guide post in our lives. Anything that goes against the promises, well, we know where that comes from and we can stand against it and win doing exactly what Jesus did, speak words of truth against our circumstances, tests, and trials. "It is written… thus-n-so, speak the promise that covers your need. We must learn to speak the Word with boldness and authority.

Did you ever notice that Jesus never said, I take authority over this matter? No, No, He simply exercised the authority He knew He already had. We need to learn to do the same thing. Why? Because Jesus didn't have anything more going for Him, than we do right now. He was not here as deity. He was here as a man, else the plan of redemption would not have worked. We have His Name, His Word, and His Spirit. If God be for us, who can "effectively" be against us? We are under authority, every name named must bow its knee to the Name of Jesus.

> Habakkuk 2:4
> Behold, his soul which is lifted up is not upright in him: but the just shall live by his faith.

This is an OT saying, but we are living in NT times.

Let me encourage you, let your inner man stand upright and be counted worthy to handle the task that is set before you.

If what is going on around you lines up with the Word, count it as a blessing. If things are not right, cast it down as from the enemy. Things like, the doctor's report, your financial statement, the fact that you don't qualify for that job that you want.

> Isaiah 54:17
> No weapon that is formed against thee shall prosper; and every tongue that shall rise against thee in judgment thou shalt condemn. This is the heritage of the servants of the LORD, and their righteousness is of me, saith the LORD.

Did you notice that we are to cast down imaginations and every high thing that exalts itself against the knowledge of God? Again, let's focus on the promises, truths, and Spiritual laws recorded in the Bible. These are our guide lines, or measuring sticks on life in this natural realm.

The Bible calls us Ambassadors for Christ. An Ambassador never gives a personal opinion. They always state the policy of the country they are from. An Ambassador doesn't live according to the laws or economy of the country they are assigned to. They live according to the laws and economy of the country they are from. They enjoy 'Diplomatic Immunity.' Though you are in the world, you are not of the world. Though your tissue type might be susceptible to cancer, or heart disease, you can, "through the knowledge of God" take a stand against these conditions and overcome them. Why? Diplomatic Immunity. Not only that but God took it a step further, God said, and thereby, …put it in motion for us.

Psalms 103:3
Who forgiveth all thine iniquities; <u>who healeth all thy diseases;</u>

Isaiah 53:5
But he was wounded for our transgressions, he was bruised for our iniquities: the chastisement of our peace was upon him; <u>and with his stripes we are healed.</u>

Matthew 8:17
That it might be fulfilled which was spoken by Esaias the prophet, saying, <u>Himself took our infirmities, and bare our sicknesses.</u>

Galatians 3:13
<u>*Christ hath redeemed us from the curse of the law,*</u> *being made a curse for us: for it is written, Cursed is every one that hangeth on a tree:*

1 Peter 2:24
Who his own self bare our sins in his own body on the tree, that we, being dead to sins, should live unto righteousness: <u>by whose stripes ye were healed.</u>

What is the curse of the law? Poverty, sickness and death.

One might say, yeah but, I've been sick many times in my life. How can I get sick if God has healed me? Good question!! Very simple,…because of a lack of knowledge.

> *Hosea 4:6a*
> *My people are destroyed for lack of knowledge…*

Remember *2 Co. 10:5*? Imaginations,…high things that exalt themselves against God's knowledge? Cast them down and take your stand!! In Faith, believing and expecting God's knowledge to overcome your circumstances, tests, and trials. THE TRUTH WILL MAKE YOU FREE, that denotes a process. Don't quit and don't give up, STAND against the wiles of the devil. And win!

Band of Believers Bible Study
► Week-2-Day-2 ◄
"Infallibility and Immutability"

We need to consider who we are dealing with. God's Word is infallible. God's Word is not subject to error, nor is it capable of failing.

> *Acts 1:3*
> *To whom also he showed himself alive after his passion by many infallible proofs, being seen of them forty days, and speaking of the things pertaining to the kingdom of God:*

Unfailing proofs, unerring proofs, and according to God's integrity, certainly not misleading proofs!

The reason we fail with God's Word, is that we are leaning on our own understanding and we are ignorant of what God has done for us. Being ignorant is sad, but being too lazy to lift a finger to find out what's wrong, and how to fix it is just plane stupid. Even irresponsibly stupid.

We have been told,

> *Romans 12:2*
> *And be not conformed to this world: but be ye transformed by the renewing of your mind, that ye may prove what is that good, and accept-*

able, and perfect, will of God.

God's Word is immutable. It is Not subject to change. Everything man has come up with is subject to change. God's Word is not subject to change, neither is there any shadow of turning.

God's Word stands, infallible and immutable!! Misleading us is not part of His plan. He gave us His Word so that we would succeed in life.

It all boils down to knowledge. As long as we try to learn about God with our carnal mind of reason, we will fail miserably. Have you ever heard the phrase, you can't get there from here? We were born with a spiritual mind. The Bible calls it, the mind of Christ in *1 Co. 2:16*. Then in:

Philippians 2:5-6
5. Let this mind be in you, which was also in Christ Jesus:
6. Who, being in the form of God, thought it not robbery to be equal with God...

Believe me, your natural mind will resist this because the things of God are foolishness to the natural mind of reason. As we grow in Spiritual knowledge, our spirits will take over our lives and we will have life and peace. It's called, putting off the old man and putting on the new man. By the way, we were told to do just that in *Eph. 4:22-24*.

Your body lives on hamburgers and fries, your intellect lives on information and experience, your Spirit lives on the Word of God.

If a person is not teachable, or willing, or inclined to renew his mind to the things of God, well, even after a thousand messages like these, that person will have learned nothing.

It all hinges on knowledge. I've been saying this for many years now, once we know how the system works, we can work the system. Do you know who you are in Christ, and do you know how the Word works?

Band of Believers Bible Study
► Week-2-Day-3 ◄
"Children of Light"

Habakkuk 2:1-4

1. I will stand upon my watch, and set me upon the tower, and will watch to see what he will say unto me, and what I shall answer when I am reproved.

2. And the LORD answered me, and said, Write the vision, and make it plain upon tables, that he may run that readeth it.

3. For the vision is yet for an appointed time, but at the end it shall speak, and not lie: though it tarry, wait for it; because it will surely come, it will not tarry.

4. Behold, his soul which is lifted up is not upright in him: but the just shall live by his faith.

We are approaching the end of the end times. I believe that God wants a band of believers who have done all to stand, so that others may see, and become embolden to take a stand themselves. I also believe that God has shown me that not all who read these messages will be able to stand. They may not be serious enough, or not even be aware that they can stand and overcome their circumstances.

Everyone wants to have the blessing of God on them, but not everyone realizes that we have a part to play in acquiring the blessings. Salvation is a done deal. Healing is a done deal. The ability to prosper is a done deal, but in all of this; there is a part for us to do in it and if we don't do it, it won't work for us. What is our part? To speak, doubt not in our heart, but believe what we said shall surely come to pass.

No one can be saved without doing their part in God's plan. No one will be healed, except they do their part.

> *Romans 1:17*
> *For therein is the righteousness of God revealed from faith to faith: as it is written, The just shall live by faith.*

From Faith unto salvation, to Faith as a way of life. We see it in Genesis. God said, and it was so. When God speaks, His Word, (the second person of the Godhead) goes out and produces what God said.

> *John 1:1-3*
> *1. In the beginning was the Word, and the Word was with God, and the Word was God.*
> *2. The same was in the beginning with God.*
> *3. All things were made by him; and without him was not any thing made that was made.*

The Word, created the sun. the Word, divided the waters and the dry land appeared. The Word, formed the animals. The power,….is in the "Word," we now call Jesus of Nazareth.

> *John 15:5*
> *I am the vine, ye are the branches: He that abideth in me, and I in him, the same bringeth forth much fruit: for without me ye can do nothing.*

Jesus just said, without me you can do nothing. Let's say it this way, without words, you can do nothing. Now in the world we have chain saws and road graders and such but in the Kingdom of God, we have only one thing. You can't see it. You can't smell it. You can't taste it, and you can't feel it, and when it is spoken, you can only hear it but for a moment as it goes out on it's way to produce what was said. Words are the only rate of exchange, the only tools we have available to us in the Kingdom of God!!

The truth shall make you free. That's always been a curious statement that Jesus made in *Jo. 8:31-32* "The truth shall make you free," that denotes a process.

God's truth, is designed to produce itself. It will save us, it will heal us, it will cause us to prosper, it will protect us, it will deliver us, and so on.

> *Hebrews 2:1-4*
> *1. Therefore we ought to give the more earnest heed to the things which we have heard, lest at any time we should let them slip.*
> *2. For if the word spoken by angels was stedfast, and every transgression and disobedience*

received a just recompense of reward;

3. How shall we escape, if we neglect so great salvation; which at the first began to be spoken by the Lord, and was confirmed unto us by them that heard him;

4. God also bearing them witness, both with signs and wonders, and with divers miracles, and gifts of the Holy Ghost, according to his own will?

Hebrews 5:12-14

12. For when for the time ye ought to be teachers, ye have need that one teach you again which be the first principles of the oracles of God; and are become such as have need of milk, and not of strong meat.

13. For every one that useth milk is unskilful in the word of righteousness: for he is a babe.

14. But strong meat belongeth to them that are of full age, even those who by reason of use have their senses exercised to discern both good and evil.

They were having trouble even in the early church. Our minds are so blinded to the truth of the Word of God that even though we want and need so much, we still don't know how to receive the help that God has already provided for us.

Hebrews 4:3b
...the works were finished from the foundation of the world.

Being an overcomer in life. For those of you who are unteachable, you're on your own, go ahead, do it your way.

> *Habakkuk 2:4*
> *Behold, his soul which is lifted up is not upright in him: but the just shall live by his faith.*

I think it's time for those who can do it, to stand upright within themselves. stand upright before our righteous God and walk as children of light, as we were instructed in ….

> *Ephesians 5:8*
> *For ye were sometimes darkness, but now are ye light in the Lord: walk as children of light:*

Everything is prepared for us, it's all already here. We must want it with all our hearts, dig deep and find it!!

> *Luke 11:9-10*
> *9. And I say unto you, Ask, and it shall be given you; seek, and ye shall find; knock, and it shall be opened unto you.*
> *10. <u>For every one that asketh receiveth; and he that seeketh findeth; and to him that knocketh it shall be opened.</u>*

God has already provided for our every need, but it is up to us to receive it. There is a way. God provided the way. Jesus said it this way, *Jo. 14:6a. I am the way, the truth, and the life:*

We need an in-depth study on the word WAY. What does it mean to us today, in the here and now. We see it first in *Isa. 35:8-10.* Then again in *Isa. 40:3-5.* and *Jer. 10:23.*

The Hebrew word used is #1870 Derek = *(deh-rek)* the part of the definition we're looking for is: Course of life, or mode of action, not journey or distance.

In the NT the word WAY appears many, many times but we're only interested in 28 listings.

It is the Greek word, #3598 Hodos = *(hod-os)* what we're looking for is mode or means, not road or distance. This word WAY, promises to be an interesting study.

Band of Believers Bible Study
► Week-2-Day-4 ◄

"Knowing How the Word Works"

John 1:1-4
1. In the beginning was the Word, and the Word was with God, and the Word was God.

2. The same was in the beginning with God.

<u>3. All things were made by him; and without him was not any thing made that was made.</u>

4. In him was life; and the life was the light of men.

If we could knew how the Word works, we might be embolden to use it in our everyday circumstances, tests, and trials. But also, in our "petition prayer time," asking God for the things we want. We need to be God-inside-minded. The Spirit of God is in you. He knows if you're praying in Faith, believing for the answer, or not. If you're believing for it, He will manifest it for you. If you're not, well, …you're going to have to go back to your Bible, stir yourself up, and pray again. If, …after you have prayed, you are expecting the answer forthwith, that's Faith!! If you're not expecting, …forget it, you're not getting anything.

Hebrews 4:12-13
12. For the word of God is quick, and pow-

erful, and sharper than any twoedged sword, piercing even to the dividing asunder of soul and spirit, and of the joints and marrow, <u>and is a discerner of the thoughts and intents of the heart.</u>

13. Neither is there any creature that is not manifest in his sight: <u>but all things are naked and opened unto the eyes of him with whom we have to do.</u>

We see in Genesis, the "Word" in action. God said, and it was so. God said, and it was so. God said, and it was so. The Word,…that is to say, the second person of the Godhead, performs the doing of whatever God says. The Word, manifests everything that God says.

Matthew 4:4
But he answered and said, <u>It is written, Man shall not live by bread alone, but by every word that proceedeth out of the mouth of God.</u>

Didn't the promises come out of the mouth of God? Think church,…the promises are God's will for His people.

1 John 5:14-15
<u>*14. And this is the confidence that we have in him, that, if we ask any thing according to his will, he heareth us:*</u>
<u>*15. And if we know that he hear us, what-*</u>

soever we ask, we know that we have the peti-
tions that we desired of him.

So how does healing manifest after we have prayed? Simple,…with signs following!!

Mark 16:20b
…the Lord working with them, and confirm-
ing the word with signs following.

Hebrews 2:4
God also bearing them witness, both with
signs and wonders, and with divers miracles, and
gifts of the Holy Ghost, according to his own will?

Let's see God's description on how the Word works.

Isaiah 55:8-11
8. For my thoughts are not your thoughts,
neither are your ways my ways, saith the LORD.
9. For as the heavens are higher than the
earth, so are my ways higher than your ways,
and my thoughts than your thoughts.
10. For as the rain cometh down, and the
snow from heaven, and returneth not thither,
but watereth the earth, and maketh it bring
forth and bud, that it may give seed to the sower,
and bread to the eater:
11. So shall my word be that goeth forth out
of my mouth: it shall not return unto me void,

but it shall accomplish that which I please, and it shall prosper in the thing whereto I sent it.

Let's go through this line by line.

11. For my thoughts are not your thoughts, neither are your ways my ways, saith the LORD.

Our goal is to learn to think the way God thinks. Renewing our minds to God's thoughts and ways. *[Ro. 12:2; Eph. 4:23; Col. 3:10]*

Once we learn how God thinks, we can see "darkly" how God does things. Before we learn how God does things, we must first learn how to speak. I know that sounds awkward but when you were a small child, you had to learn how to talk,…didn't you? Until we learn how God thinks, we cannot form words and sentences. We'll talk about verse 9 in a few minutes.

10. For as the rain cometh down, and the snow from heaven, and returneth not thither, but watereth the earth, and maketh it bring forth and bud, that it may give seed to the sower, and bread to the eater:

Rain is designed to make things grow. It is not designed to fall to the earth, evaporate and go back to the atmosphere. and returneth not thither. Rain waters the earth so that it brings forth and buds. That's why we have grass, trees, wheat and barley. Things can't grow without water!!

> *11. So shall my word be that goeth forth out of my mouth: it shall not return unto me void, but it shall accomplish that which I please, and it shall prosper in the thing whereto I sent it.*

God's Word is given,…to produce something. What is it supposed to produce? How about,… exactly what it says or describes. *By whose stripes, ye were healed*, is designed to effect healing. Calling on the name of the Lord, is designed to save us. *Whatsoever we do shall prosper*, is designed to prosper us no matter what business endeavor we want to get involved in.

Come on church, think. We've been set up in a most excellent way, the promises that are recorded in the Bible. They are designed to produce or manifest themselves through our Faith. Jesus went about doing good and healing the sick for who knows how long, but the day came when He said, *"Woman, thy Faith has made you whole."* We have a part to play in this. What is our part? To speak, believing what we said shall surely come to pass. Listen to this…

> *John 14:13*
> *13. And whatsoever ye shall ask in my name, that will I do, that the Father may be glorified in the Son.*
> *14. If ye shall ask any thing in my name, I will do it.*

We saw earlier that Jesus, "The Word" does everything that God says, Right? Well now we see that Jesus, "The Word" will do whatsoever WE ask, in His name!! He will do it!! How cool is that? We're going to have to get on the other side of this learning curve in order to do it consistently. We must first learn how to think, then speak words, and then,…exercise wisdom.

You are not alone. Jesus is in your heart, He knows what you're thinking, and He knows what you intend to do when you get your desired result from your prayer. He knows when you're believing for it, and He knows when you're not. If you're expecting, …THAT'S FAITH!!

Band of Believers Bible Study
► Week-2-Day-5 ◄
"A No-Nonsense Attitude"

2 Timothy 2:1-7

1. Thou therefore, my son, be strong in the grace that is in Christ Jesus.

2. And the things that thou hast heard of me among many witnesses, the same commit thou to faithful men, who shall be able to teach others also.

3. Thou therefore endure hardness, as a good soldier of Jesus Christ.

4. No man that warreth entangleth himself with the affairs of this life; that he may please him who hath chosen him to be a soldier.

5. And if a man also strive for masteries, yet is he not crowned, except he strive lawfully.

6. The husbandman that laboureth must be first partaker of the fruits.

7. Consider what I say; and the Lord give thee understanding in all things.

If we are going to walk in the knowledge of God, and live out our lives according to Kingdom Rule on the earth, we must do it lawfully. We must do it according to how God has set up the WAY, the Truth, and the Life. FAITH is the only way we can exercise the power of the Word, in the Kingdom.

2 Tim. 2:1-7 doesn't say it like I would like it said, but it is in the ballpark. Attitude, purpose and determination, must accompany our spoken words if we hope for them to come to pass. In other words, mean what you say when you say it. If you say it right, Jesus will confirm your words with signs following.

Now that you know how the system works, WORK THE SYSTEM!!

(v. 7) ___Consider what I say; and the Lord give thee understanding in all things.___

Ephesians 6:10
___Finally, my brethren, be strong in the Lord, and in the power of his might.___

You have the "Power of Attorney." You stand in the place of Jesus on the earth.

Matthew 28:18-20
18. And Jesus came and spake unto them, saying, All power is given unto me in heaven and in earth.

19. Go ye therefore, and teach all nations, baptizing them in the name of the Father, and of the Son, and of the Holy Ghost:

20. Teaching them to observe all things whatsoever I have commanded you: and, lo, I am with you alway, even unto the end of the world. Amen.

If you're a wimp, or not serious enough, don't try this at home. You have learned just enough to get into trouble. One doesn't try Faith. One does Faith, by speaking, doubting not, but believing that what one says shall come to pass. Isn't that what Jesus said in…

Matthew 21:21-22

21. Jesus answered and said unto them, Verily I say unto you, If ye have faith, and doubt not, ye shall not only do this which is done to the fig tree, but also if ye shall say unto this mountain, Be thou removed, and be thou cast into the sea; <u>it shall be done.</u>

<u>22. And all things, whatsoever ye shall ask in prayer, believing, ye shall receive.</u>

Mark 11:23-24

23. For verily I say unto you, That whosoever shall say unto this mountain, Be thou removed, and be thou cast into the sea; and shall not doubt in his heart, but shall believe that those things which he saith shall come to pass; he shall have whatsoever he saith.

<u>24. Therefore I say unto you, What things soever ye desire, when ye pray, believe that ye receive them, and ye shall have them.</u>

We are in charge, we have the Authority. We have God's Word, use it, use it with the same confidence that you would use as if Jesus was standing here praying for you.

1 John 5:13-15

13. *These things have I written unto you that believe on the name of the Son of God; that ye may know that ye have eternal life, and that ye may believe on the name of the Son of God.*

14. *And this is the confidence that we have in him, that, if we ask any thing according to his will, he heareth us:*

15. *And if we know that he hear us, whatsoever we ask, we know that we have the petitions that we desired of him.*

Luke 12:32

Fear not, little flock; for it is your Father's good pleasure to give you the kingdom.

REVIEWING WEEK 2

1. No matter what we see, hear or feel one thing reigns over all. What is it?_____

2. Ambassadors live according to the laws and economy of the country they are from, because they enjoy
_____?

3. Jesus came to earth as a mere man, without any special powers or advantages.   TRUE or FALSE

4. God's truth, is designed to do what? _____
_____

What is our part? _____
_____

5. (From Week 2 Day 4) Complete the following sentence: We see in Genesis, the "_____" in action. God _____, and it was so. God _____, and it was so. God _____, and it was so.

6. The promises of the Bible are designed to produce or manifest themselves through what?_____
How, please explain?_____
_____
_____
_____

7. We have God's Word, we are in charge, we have the Authority; we have been given the "_____
_____."

■ NOTES ■

Band of Believers Bible Study
► Additional Notes 1 ◄
"Principalities and Powers"

I like something that Jesus said in...

> *Mark 4:21-24*
> *21. And he said unto them, Is a candle brought to be put under a bushel, or under a bed? and not to be set on a candlestick?*
> *22. For there is nothing hid, which shall not be manifested; neither was any thing kept secret, but that it should come abroad.*
> *23. If any man have ears to hear, let him hear.*
> *24. And he said unto them, Take heed what ye hear: with what measure ye mete, it shall be measured to you: and unto you that hear shall more be given.*

If you measure this to be talking to Cyrus only, you will be missing out on the blessing. If however, you measure this to be instruction...

> *2 Timothy 3:16-17*
> *16. All scripture is given by inspiration of God, and is profitable for doctrine, for reproof, for correction, for instruction in righteousness:*
> *17. That the man of God may be perfect,*

thoroughly furnished unto all good works.

Yes, God was talking to Cyrus yesterday, but isn't He talking to you today too? Let's see what this scripture is saying to us today through the mind of the Spirit, not the mind of the flesh.

Let's take a serious look at...

> *Isaiah 45:2-3*
> *2. I will go before thee, and make the crooked places straight: I will break in pieces the gates of brass, and cut in sunder the bars of iron:*
> *3. And I will give thee the treasures of darkness, and hidden riches of secret places, that thou mayest know that I, the LORD, which call thee by thy name, am the God of Israel.*

We just saw this earlier, when we speak "the Word" or the promise that covers our need, the word goes before us and makes a way for us. *[Isa. 35:8-10, 40:3-4]*

And I will give thee the treasures of darkness,

The Hebrew word for *treasures*: denotes a storehouse, or depository.

The Hebrew word for *darkness*: denotes a state of being unknown.

...and hidden riches of secret places

The Hebrew word for *hidden*: denotes buried money, hidden riches, treasure.

The Hebrew word for *riches*: denotes a secret storehouse, a secreted valuable (buried) money, hidden riches, (hid) treasure (-s).

The Hebrew word for *secret*: denotes concealed, covert, secret place

The word for *places* is not defined in Strong's Concordance, but we get the inference, something buried in the ground.

...that thou mayest know that I, the LORD,
which call thee by thy name, am the God of Israel.

Why does God do this? To show Himself as God, ...your God, Who calls you by name and prepares the way for you though you have not known Him, in time past, ...you know Him now.

So, ...what's my point in all this? Well, to the carnal mind, this explanation is going to sound pretty far fetched, even foolishness. Having been a prospector in early life, I can appreciate this scripture more than others. I still have several gold panning pans, a four foot hand sluice box, and a variety of rock breaking hand tools, shovels and two metal detectors.

To me, ...this Scripture shows me that I don't have to "pay my dues" anymore. By that I mean, I don't have to put in a lot of time for weeks and months in order to find the treasure I'm looking for. God will show me where to dig and how deep. What used to take weeks or months can now be done in 20 minutes or an hour.

I choose to have success God's way, not the old familiar trial and error methods of man's ways.

> *Take heed what ye hear: with what measure*
> *ye mete, it shall be measured to you.*

THAT'S POWER!! DIVINE POWER,..."WORD" POWER!! "The Word" I'm speaking of is a person,... the second person of the Godhead.

> *John 1:1-4*
> *1. In the beginning was the Word, and the Word was with God, and the Word was God.*
> *2. The same was in the beginning with God.*
> *3. All things were made by him; and without him was not any thing made that was made.*
> *4. In him was life; and the life was the light of men.*

Jesus, "The Word," in His primary identity, performs the doing of everything God says. We see it clearly in *Gen. 1:1-31.* Then Jesus said in

> *John 14:13-14*
> *13. And whatsoever ye shall ask in my name, that will I do, that the Father may be glorified in the Son.*
> *14. If ye shall ask any thing in my name, I will do it.*

So, we see that Jesus, "The Word" performs the doing of what God says AND, He will perform the doing of anything we ask for, …in His Name. How cool is that? This learning curve is not so difficult is it!! All we need do is purpose in our hearts and determine to be diligent and press in. Press into what? The knowledge of The Kingdom of God.

All the road blocks and circumstances that principalities and powers and rulers of darkness can try to put in our way can be circumvented, by-passed and overcome by the Word of God on our behalf.

Let's face it folks, the most consistent enemy we have is our own carnal thinking of our own selves. Yes, there are principalities and powers set in place by the devil to harass us and their ability to deceive and mislead us is formidable. That doesn't take away from the fact that we are our own worst enemy. Until we renew our minds from the way the old man thinks and does things, to the way God is trying to teach us to think and do things, we have an ongoing problem.

God is not going to renew our minds for us like He did for the craftsmen who built the Tabernacle and the Ark of the covenant. God told us to renew our minds. The time is coming that we will know even as we are known, but that time has not yet come. God will not cross your will. God has given us everything we need, but if we don't partake,…well who else can we blame?

You are in charge of your life! If you knew that,… things would be different wouldn't they?!

Everybody's waiting and wanting God to do something in their lives. In case you haven't noticed, God hasn't done all that much about your circumstances lately. Without Faith, it's impossible to please Him.

Why do you think Jesus said,

Matthew 10-24-25a
24. The disciple is not above his master, nor the servant above his lord.
25. It is enough for the disciple that he be as his master, and the servant as his lord…

You have a part to play. God has given us all we need to succeed, we have His Word, His Name, His Spirit, and the authority to use them at will. Why would we ask God to reach down and touch someone when He has told us to do it? YOU, lay hands on the sick, and they shall recover. YOU, pray the prayer of Faith and change things. YOU, call things that be not as though they were. This is not rocket science, when we see it and accept it, it's child's play, so simple.

The ball is in your court. Are you going to act accordingly, or just cry and whine and complain and beg God to do something on your behalf? Grow up!! YOU, are in charge!! DO something!!

Band of Believers Bible Study
► Additional Notes 2 ◄
"To The Intent"

A few days ago I posted Week-1-day-5 "To The Intent" It is one of the shortest chapters in the book. The Lord has been dealing with me to reiterate, and go over it again because without "intent" our words will fall to the ground. "To the intent," is crucial to success.

God gave us promises, "to the intent" that the promises He gave us would produce the desired result of what the promises say or describe. The promise is like a seed. It has all the information in the seed, to produce the desired result.

When we speak a promise of God, "to the intent" of being healed, or delivered, or saved, or whatever, if there is no "intent" our Faith has nothing to work with. You're still just-a-hopein-and-a-prayin. Not in a mode of EXPECTATION. Intent, …focuses our prayer. Faith, …lends substance to our prayers. Expectation, …is a receiver of the desired result, …of our prayers.

When we apply all three, INTENT, FAITH, & EXPECTATION, God will move mountians to get to you to answer your prayer with signs following, according to His riches in glory by The Word!! No, I didn't misquote that Scripture, …Jesus, is The Word, in person. God watches over His Word, to perform it.

I've said it before, and I will say it again, we need to mean what we say!! EXPECTING,… until our words come to pass. If we're not expecting,…our receiver is not turned on.

Let me share the latest revelation God gave me just last week. The imagination, whether it be God's imagination or mans imagination, whether it be a born again man or a heathen man, doesn't seem to matter. The imagination…. is the womb of creativity. It is in the imagination that we form and shape our wants and desires.

> *Jeremiah 1:5a*
> *Before I formed thee in the belly I knew thee; and before thou camest forth out of the womb I sanctified thee...*

As we speak, …our wants and desires come forth in the form of words. Words are like seeds. They have all the information in them that is necessary to produce what we said.

> *John 14:13-14*
> *13. And whatsoever ye shall ask in my name, that will I do, that the Father may be glorified in the Son.*
> *14. If ye shall ask any thing in my name, I will do it.*

> *John 15:7*
> *If ye abide in me, and my words abide in you,*

ye shall ask what ye will, and it shall be done unto you.

Jesus working with us confirming our words with signs following.

> *1 John 5:14-15*
> *14. And this is the confidence that we have in him, that, if we ask any thing according to his will, he heareth us:*
> *15. And if we know that he hear us, whatsoever we ask, we know that we have the petitions that we desired of him.*

The promises are God's will for His people. Duhhhhhh. Come on church, think! Our desires are formed in our imagination, ...when we speak them "to the intent" of them coming to pass, ...our Faith, gives them substance even though the desires are not yet seen.

> *Philippians 2:5-6*
> *5. Let this mind be in you, which was also in Christ Jesus:*
> *6. Who, being in the form of God, thought it not robbery to be equal with God:*

We are children of the Most High. Act like it!! Walk as children of Light.

Band of Believers Bible Study
▶ Additional Notes 3 ◀
"Practical Application"

Sometimes I'm a little slow on the uptake, naive, and somewhat too dense to take advantage of new information. With that in mind, I would like to give some practical application suggestions on how to use The Word, …in time of need. Since the curse of the Law covers the most important issues of life, I will primarily deal with it, Poverty, Sickness, and Death. All other issues of life can be dealt with …the same way, Okay?

The Bible says that we have already overcome the world. How did we do it? We received Jesus as saviour, and were born again, IN HIM. Our life is hid in Him. It is a mystery hidden in God.

Mark 4:11-12

11. And He said unto them, Unto you it is given to know the mystery of the kingdom of God: but unto them that are without, all these things are done in parables:

12. That seeing they may see, and not perceive; and hearing they may hear, and not understand; lest at any time they should be converted, and their sins should be forgiven them.

There you go, …now we are born again and alive before God, …Spiritually, AND …we were given

The Righteousness which is of God, through Grace, not having to establish our own righteousness which is of The Law of Moses.

> *John 1:17*
> *For the law was given by Moses, but grace and truth came by Jesus Christ.*

SO, …how did we do this? If God wanted us saved, He could have done it by Himself, Right? Wrong!! God gave us a free will. God will not over-ride our free will to chose. He doesn't want a bunch of puppets. He wants a people that want Him as their God. So, obviously …we had a part to play in His plan of redemption, and The Word had it's part to play too. The Word, the second person of the Godhead was made flesh,…

> *John 1:14*
> *And the Word was made flesh, and dwelt among us, (and we beheld his glory, the glory as of the only begotten of the Father,) full of grace and truth.*

Before Mathew, Mark, Luke, and John, we had The Father, The Word, and The Spirit, …but now we have The Father, The Son, and The Holy Ghost. Jesus, "the man" had a beginning just like we did. He was born here.

Before He was born here, He was "The Word of God."

John 1:1-4

1. In the beginning was the Word, and the Word was with God, and the Word was God.

2. The same was in the beginning with God.

3. All things were made by him; and without him was not any thing made that was made.

4. In him was life; and the life was the light of men.

Jeremiah 10:23

O LORD, I know that the way of man is not in himself: it is not in man that walketh to direct his steps.

When we received Jesus as saviour, we received "The Way," of life for mankind. Jesus put it this way,...

John 14:6

I am the way, the truth, and the life: no man cometh unto the Father, but by me.

Habakkuk 2:4

Behold, his soul which is lifted up is not up-right in him: but the just shall live by his faith.

Hab. 2:4 apply describes the Church today. God has lifted us up but the Church teaches that we are so unworthy.

So what was our part to play in God's plan? We were to believe, and confess that, ...Jesus is The Christ, and ask Him to save us, Right? Isn't that what we did? We believed the report that Jesus is the Christ, and we asked Him into our hearts and save us!! That's it? YES, that's it!! We heard the report, doubted not in our hearts but believed what we were saying would come to pass. Jesus said that for anyone that would do that, ...will have what they said. AND, you're still saying it today ...I'm Saved!!

Guess what, that's the way things are done in The Kingdom of God. God speaks, and what God said, ...comes to pass. The second person of the Godhead, performs the doing of what God said. God said, LIGHT BE, The Word, went out and created the sun.

Man was created in God's image and after His likeness. When we received Jesus as saviour, we received "The Way" of mankind. It is because of the Righteousness of God given to us at the new birth that when we speak of Faith,... "The Word," performs the doing of what we said, and I can prove it!!!

> *John 14:13-14*
> *13. And whatsoever ye shall ask in my name, that will I do, that the Father may be glorified in the Son.*
> *14. If ye shall ask any thing in my name, I will do it.*

So we asked Jesus to save us, and He did. How did we do it? By speaking words, doubting not, but believing what we said shall come to pass.

Now, let's look at poverty and sickness. We should

have learned this "principle" when we were born again, but we're slow and possibly stupid, so we missed it. God gave us the promise of salvation. We believed it and said some words to establish the fact that we received the promise that God promised. Get it? Sooooo, in order to receive any degree of prosperity at all, we need to agree with what God has already said about prosperity, Right?

> *Psalm 1:1-3*
> *1. Blessed is the man that walketh not in the counsel of the ungodly, nor standeth in the way of sinners, nor sitteth in the seat of the scornful.*
> *2. But his delight is in the law of the LORD; and in his law doth he meditate day and night.*
> *3. And he shall be like a tree planted by the rivers of water, that bringeth forth his fruit in his season; his leaf also shall not wither; and whatsoever he doeth shall prosper.*

> *Philippians 4:19*
> *But my God shall supply all your need according to his riches in glory by Christ Jesus.*

Again, who is Christ Jesus? The Word, ...The Way of man. Okay now, how can we apply this information?

Let's use a business scenario, or buying your own house, or making sure that your child has a college education.

It doesn't really matter what you're believing for, the

"principle" works the same "way." Get it...."WAY"?

> *Isaiah 55:1-3*
>
> *1. Ho, every one that thirsteth, come ye to the waters, and he that hath no money; come ye, buy, and eat; yea, come, buy wine and milk without money and without price.*
>
> *2. Wherefore do ye spend money for that which is not bread? and your labour for that which satisfieth not? hearken diligently unto me, and eat ye that which is good, and let your soul delight itself in fatness.*
>
> *3. Incline your ear, and come unto me: hear, and your soul shall live; and I will make an everlasting covenant with you, even the sure mercies of David.*

This is The Kingdom of God we're talking about, not this natural realm. You built your business by framing it with words at the prayer meeting, or in your own private prayer time. Without money, and without price. Just like God did in Genesis chapter one when God framed the creation and restoration of earth. He did it without money and without price by using WORDS!! Describing what He wanted, and "The Word" of God, ...we now call Jesus, performed the doing of what God said.

It doesn't matter if you're asking for a box of tissue or a multimillion dollar office building. We receive it even as we're asking for it. Without money and without price.

God does these things according to His riches in

Glory....by The Word!! Not our bank account!!! His!!! When the harvest time comes, the money will be there waiting for you.

> *Matthew 21:22*
> *And all things, whatsoever ye shall ask in prayer, believing, ye shall receive.*

> *Mark 11:24*
> *Therefore I say unto you, What things soever ye desire, when ye pray, believe that ye receive them, and ye shall have them.*

Why?

> *Mark 4:26-29*
> *26. So is the kingdom of God, as if a man should cast seed into the ground;*
> *27. And should sleep, and rise night and day, and the seed should spring and grow up, he knoweth not how.*
> *28. For the earth bringeth forth fruit of herself; first the blade, then the ear, after that the full corn in the ear.*
> *29. But when the fruit is brought forth, immediately he putteth in the sickle, because the harvest is come.*

In The Kingdom of God, WORDS are SEEDS. Seeds are designed to produce, and in Genesis, we see that every seed will produce after its own kind. That means that every promise of God is capable to produce what it states or describes. For you computer geeks out there, Jesus is our Word Prossessor.

> *John 14:14*
> *If ye shall ask any thing in my name, I will do it.*

Just like Jesus did in Genesis for God when God formed the creation with words? YES, just like He did in Genesis, *for without Him was not anything made that was made.*

I know I repeat myself a lot, but that's part of the teaching. You didn't learn the multiplication table in one day and you're not going to learn this in one hearing either.

> *Isaiah 28:9-13*
> *9. Whom shall he teach knowledge? and whom shall he make to understand doctrine? them that are weaned from the milk, and drawn from the breasts.*
> *10. For precept must be upon precept, precept upon precept; line upon line, line upon line; here a little, and there a little:*
> *11. For with stammering lips and another tongue will he speak to this people.*
> *12. To whom he said, This is the rest wherewith ye may cause the weary to rest; and this is*

the refreshing: yet they would not hear.

13. But the word of the LORD was unto them precept upon precept, precept upon precept; line upon line, line upon line; here a little, and there a little; that they might go, and fall backward, and be broken, and snared, and taken.

Did you notice, This is the rest wherewith ye may cause the weary to rest; and this is the refreshing: When we speak The Word, or our own words, we may now enter into God's rest, EXPPECTING, until our words come to pass. As a man sows seed into the ground, sleeps and rises night and day…

Now, let's talk about healing, we have a part to play. We need to agree with what God has said about healing, Right? Okay.

Psalm 103:1-5

1. Bless the LORD, O my soul: and all that is within me, bless his holy name.

2. Bless the LORD, O my soul, and forget not all his benefits:

3. Who forgiveth all thine iniquities; who healeth all thy diseases;

4. Who redeemeth thy life from destruction; who crowneth thee with lovingkindness and tender mercies;

5. Who satisfieth thy mouth with good things; so that thy youth is renewed like the eagle's.

Isaiah 53:4-5

4. Surely he hath borne our griefs, and carried our sorrows: yet we did esteem him stricken, smitten of God, and afflicted.

5. But he was wounded for our transgressions, he was bruised for our iniquities: the chastisement of our peace was upon him; and with his stripes we are healed.

Matthew 8:17

That it might be fulfilled which was spoken by Esaias the prophet, saying, Himself took our infirmities, and bare our sicknesses.

1 Peter 2:24-25

24. Who his own self bare our sins in his own body on the tree, that we, being dead to sins, should live unto righteousness: by whose stripes ye were healed.

25. For ye were as sheep going astray; but are now returned unto the Shepherd and Bishop of your souls.

David says in the twenty-third Psalm.

Psalm 23:5

Thou preparest a table before me in the presence of mine enemies:

We may not realize it but Divine Health is on the

table. All we have to do to receive it, is to speak it, doubt not in our hearts, but believe we receive it, and by and by, we shall have it. As a man casts seed into the ground....

Your Divine health will come unannounced, it will come up from behind you and overtake you and you will be Cadillacing along and suddenly realize that you haven't been sick in a long, long time. Even the symptoms of that condition you had are now ...somehow ...gone. Hey, what a deal ...that just goes to show that The Word Works!!

Band of Believers Bible Study
► Additional Notes 4 ◄

"Preventive Maintenance"

Preventive Maintenance is "Very Important!"

Before my wife and I were married, she told me that she used to have a problem with air conditioning in the summer. Her sinuses would fill up and block her nose. She said that she got the revelation to address the summer problem in the winter, and any winter problems, in the summer by sowing words to take care of them ahead of time. As a man sows seed in the ground... What a most excellent idea!! Knowing how the Kingdom works. Knowing that our words are as seeds. Knowing that a seed has to have time to grow and produce the fruit. A daily confession just may be an excellent way of life for us who know the truth. You know, ...the truth that makes us free!?!?

Somebody needs to write a book of daily confessions so that we can "according to knowledge" bring down the high places, build up the low places, straighten out the kinks, and smooth out the rough places on our path of life. Kinda sounds like the road that John built, doesn't it?

Isaiah 40:3-5
3. The voice of him that crieth in the wilder-

ness, Prepare ye the way of the LORD, make straight in the desert a highway for our God.

4. Every valley shall be exalted, and every mountain and hill shall be made low: and the crooked shall be made straight, and the rough places plain:

5. And the glory of the LORD shall be revealed, and all flesh shall see it together: for the mouth of the LORD hath spoken it.

According to *Matthew 4:4 We are to live by every word that proceeds out of the mouth of God.*

Matthew 3:1-3

1. In those days came John the Baptist, preaching in the wilderness of Judaea,

2. And saying, Repent ye: for the kingdom of heaven is at hand.

3. For this is he that was spoken of by the prophet Esaias, saying, The voice of one crying in the wilderness, Prepare ye the way of the Lord, make his paths straight.

We don't have to go to Jerusalem to pray or be prayed for, we don't have to recite any oaths to God in order to get our prayers answered. *Speak the Word only and my servant will be healed!!!* Whoa, …Son, WHAT GREAT FAITH YOU HAVE!!

A daily confession would be different than a daily Devotional. A daily devotional is an inspiring message.

A daily confession can most certainly be accompanied by a demonstration of the Spirit, and Power.

> *1 Corinthians 2:3-7*
> *3. And I was with you in weakness, and in fear, and in much trembling.*
> *4. And my speech and my preaching was not with enticing words of man's wisdom, but in demonstration of the Spirit and of power:*
> *5. That your faith should not stand in the wisdom of men, but in the power of God.*
> *6. Howbeit we speak wisdom among them that are perfect: yet not the wisdom of this world, nor of the princes of this world, that come to nought:*
> *7. But we speak the wisdom of God in a mystery, even the hidden wisdom, which God ordained before the world unto our glory:*

If you want your own house, start talking about it, frame it with words just like God did in Genesis. Then enter into God's rest, believing that Jesus is working with you confirming your words with signs following.

> *John 4:35a*
> *Say not ye, There are yet four months, and then cometh harvest?...*

> *Hebrews 10:23*
> *Let us hold fast the profession of our faith with-*

out wavering; (for he is faithful that promised;)

Hebrews 12:1-3
1. Wherefore seeing we also are compassed about with so great a cloud of witnesses, let us lay aside every weight, and the sin which doth so easily beset us, and let us run with patience the race that is set before us,

2. Looking unto Jesus the author and finisher of our faith; who for the joy that was set before him endured the cross, despising the shame, and is set down at the right hand of the throne of God.

Jesus said,
John 14:13-14
13. And whatsoever ye shall ask in my name, that will I do, that the Father may be glorified in the Son.

14. If ye shall ask any thing in my name, I will do it.

Through the promises, God has made provision for anything that can come against us in the world. Are you going to hunker down and take everything that life in this natural realm has to throw at you, or are you going to take charge by,

2 Corinthians 10:5-6
5. Casting down imaginations, and every high thing that exalteth itself against the knowl-

edge of God, and bringing into captivity every thought to the obedience of Christ;

6. And having in a readiness to revenge all disobedience, when your obedience is fulfilled.

Can you take your stand, make your confession, and hang in there for four months? A seed never looks like the plant. The fruit of the plant never looks like the plant. Inside the fruit is more seed, an abundance of seed, enough for everyone!! We will never run out of WORDS!! Words are the only rate of exchange in The Kingdom of God. No Money, no Silver, no Gold. It's words only in The Kingdom of God, a never ending supply, OUR WEALTH, …IS IN THE WORDS WE SPEAK, DOUBT NOT, BUT BELIEVE THEY WILL PRODUCE THE FRUIT OF WHAT WE SAID!!

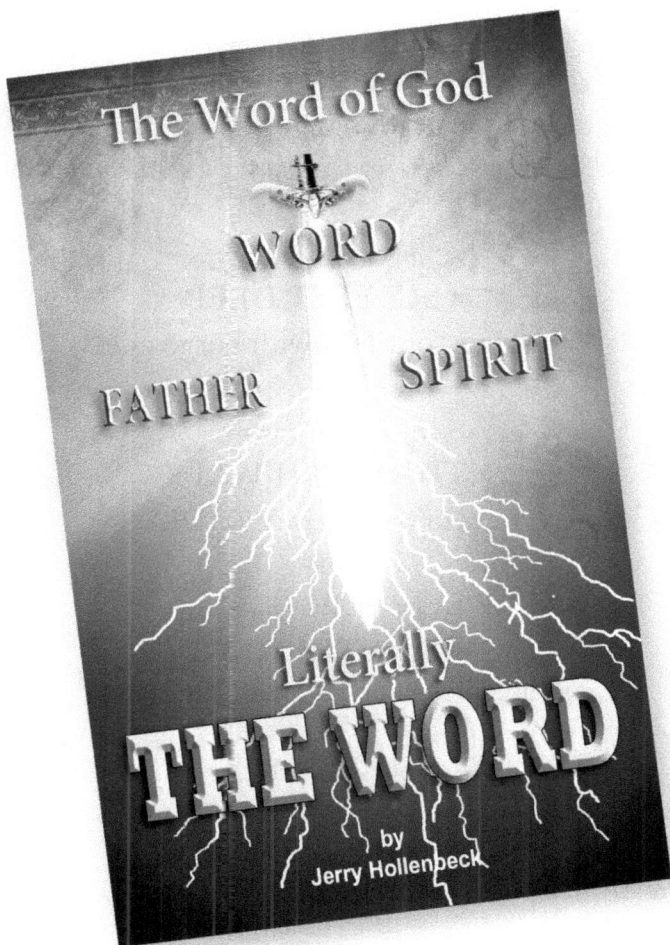

Check out these other Great Books from
BOLD TRUTH PUBLISHING

by Adrienne Gottlieb
• The Replacement Theology LIE
The Book Jews wished every Christian would read

----

by Daryl Holloman
• Seemed Good to The Holy Ghost
Inspired Teachings by Brother Daryl
PLUS - Prophecies spoken in Pardo, Cebu, Philippines

----

by Steve Young
• SIX FEET DEEP
Burying Your Past with Forgiveness

----

by Paul Howard
• THE FAITH WALK
Keys to walking in VICTORY!

----

by Joe Waggnor
• Bless THE KING
Praise Poems for My Lord and Saviour

----

by Ed Marr
• C. H. P.
Coffee Has Priority
The Memoirs of a California Highway Patrol - Badge 9045

• FREEDOM
The Liberty that Repentance Brings
An Investigation of True Repentance

by Jerry W. Hollenbeck
• The KINGDOM of GOD
An Agrarian Society
Featuring The Kingdom Realities, Bible Study Course,
Research and Development Classes

• The Word of God
FATHER • WORD • SPIRIT
Literally THE WORD

----

by Mary Ann England
• Women in Ministry
From her Teachings at the FCF Bible School - Tulsa, Oklahoma
Compiled and Edited by Charles R. England
(Foreword by Pat Harrison)

----

by James Jonsten
• WHO is GOD to YOU?
The path to know the most misunderstood name in the universe.

----

by Martha (Marti) McNabb
• The POWER of GOD
The Power of God will help us to live in
The Kingdom of God while we are here on the Earth

----

by Aaron Jones
• In the SECRET PLACE of THE MOST HIGH
God's Word for Supernatural Healing, Deliverance and Protection

• SOUND from HEAVEN
Praying in Tongues for a Victorious Life

Available at Select Bookstores and
www.BOLDTRUTHPUBLISHING.com

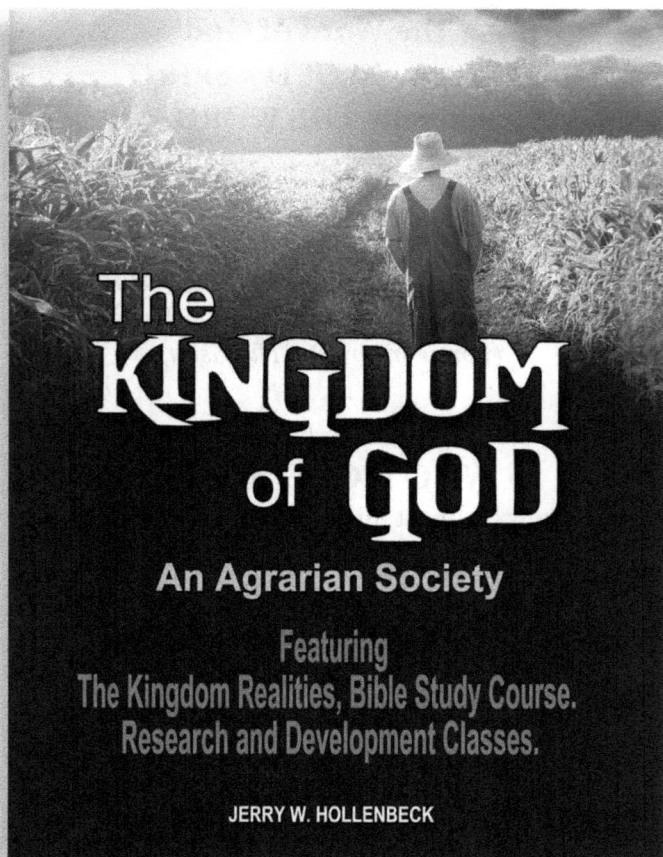

www.ingramcontent.com/pod-product-compliance
Lightning Source LLC
Chambersburg PA
CBHW071008040426
42443CB00007B/714